Pebble® Plus

Let's Celebrate

Earth Day

APRIL

by Clara Cella

Consulting Editor: Gail Saunders-Smith, PhD

CAPSTONE PRESS
a capstone imprint

Pebble Plus is published by Capstone Press,
1710 Roe Crest Drive, North Mankato, Minnesota 56003.
www.capstonepub.com

Library of Congress Cataloging-in-Publication Data
Cella, Clara.
Earth day / by Clara Cella.
p. cm. — (Pebble plus. Let's celebrate)
Includes index.
Summary: "Full-color photographs and simple text provide a brief introduction to Earth Day"—Provided
by publisher.
ISBN 978-1-4296-8730-0 (library binding)
ISBN 978-1-4296-9384-4 (paperback)
ISBN 978-1-62065-305-0 (ebook PDF)
1. Earth Day—Juvenile literature. I. Title.

GE195.5C45 2013
394.262—dc23   2012003828

Editorial Credits
Jill Kalz, editor; Kyle Grenz, designer; Marcie Spence, media researcher; Kathy McColley, production specialist

Photo Credits
AP Images: 15, CWH, 13 (left); Capstone Studio: Karon Dubke, 5, 7 (all), 17, 19, 21, 22; iStockphoto: JackJM, 9;
    Shutterstock: Christian Delbert, cover (lightbulb), Gelpi, cover (girl), grynold, 11, kk-artworks, 1, RTimages, cover
    (recycling bin); Wisconsin Historical Society, Image Number 93130, 13 (right)

Note to Parents and Teachers

The Let's Celebrate series supports curriculum standards for social studies related to culture.
This book describes and illustrates the Earth Day holiday. The images support early readers in
understanding the text. The repetition of words and phrases helps early readers learn new words.
This book also introduces early readers to subject-specific vocabulary words, which are defined
in the Glossary section. Early readers may need assistance to read some words and to use the
Table of Contents, Glossary, Read More, Internet Sites, and Index sections of the book.

Printed in the United States of America in North Mankato, Minnesota.

112012   007045R

Table of Contents

Hello, Earth Day!

Earth Day is a time
to celebrate our planet.
The holiday happens
every year on April 22.

Earth is full of life.

Fish swim. Birds fly.

Plants bloom. People, pets,

and wild animals play!

All life on Earth needs
clean air and water.
It's our job to take care
of the planet. Earth Day
reminds us of this duty.

How It Began

Gaylord Nelson started Earth Day.
Nelson was a lawmaker
from Wisconsin. He worried
about pollution and what it
was doing to our planet.

Nelson got help from a man named Denis Hayes. Together they planned the first Earth Day. Millions of people celebrated it on April 22, 1970.

Gaylord Nelson

Denis Hayes

13

People gathered in parks and along streets. They gave speeches. Lawmakers listened and went on to pass laws to protect the environment.

Let's Celebrate!

It's Earth Day!

How will you celebrate?

Pick up litter. Toss cans,

bottles, and newspapers

in recycling bins.

Plant trees for Earth Day.
Trees help clean the air.
They take harmful materials
out of the air. They also
help clean the dirt.

19

Save energy on Earth Day.

Turn off the lights

when you leave a room.

Use a bike instead of a car.

Show Earth you care!

Activity: Recycle That!

People in the United States use about 4 million plastic bottles—every hour! But only one in four is recycled. Millions of bottles lie useless in landfills. Do your part to help. Start a recycling program at your house.

What You Need:

paper

scissors

a marker

tape

4 plastic tubs

What You Do:

1. Use the paper and scissors to make four labels.

2. Mark the labels "paper," "plastic," "glass," and "aluminum."

3. Tape one label on each tub.

4. Have your family sort their trash into the tubs. Then have your mom or dad find out where to take the materials.

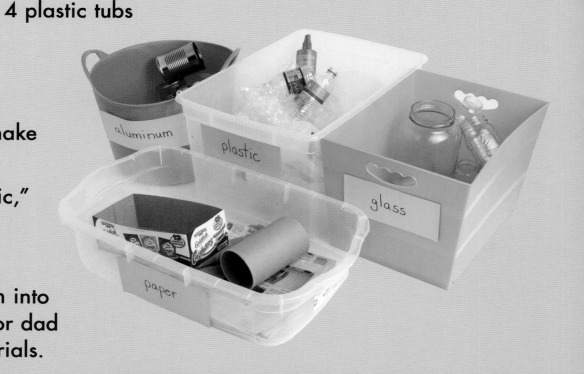

Read More

Aloian, Molly. *Earth Day.* Celebrations in My World. New York: Crabtree, 2009.

Rissman, Rebecca. *Earth Day.* Holidays and Festivals. Chicago: Heinemann Library, 2011.

Trueit, Trudi Strain. *Earth Day.* Rookie Read-About Holidays. New York: Children's Press, 2007.

Internet Sites

FactHound offers a safe, fun way to find Internet sites related to this book. All of the sites on FactHound have been researched by our staff.

Here's all you do:

Visit *www.facthound.com*

Type in this code: 9781429687300

Check out projects, games and lots more at
www.capstonekids.com

23

Glossary

celebrate—to honor someone or something on a special day

environment—all of the trees, plants, water, and dirt

pollution—materials that hurt Earth's water, air, and land

recycling—the process of using things again instead of throwing them away

Index

activities, 14, 16, 18, 20
air, 8, 18
animals, 6
dates, 4, 12

Hayes, Denis, 12
history of holiday, 10, 12, 14
Nelson, Gaylord, 10, 12
plants, 6, 18
water, 8

Word Count: 196
Grade: 1
Early-Intervention Level: 19